D1707371

Abattoir

Abattoir

Angelo Mao

Winner of the 2019 Burnside Review Press Book Award
Selected by Darcie Dennigan

Burnside Review Press   Portland, Oregon

Abattoir
© 2021 Angelo Mao

Cover Image: Mu Pan, *Small Rabbits*

Cover Design: Susie Steele
Layout: Zach Grow

Printed in the U.S.A.
First Edition, 2021
ISBN: 978-0-9992649-7-3

Burnside Review Press
Portland, Oregon
www.burnsidereview.org

Burnside Review Press titles are available for purchase from the
publisher and Small Press Distribution (www.spdbooks.org).

for my husband

I.

II.

III.

IV.

Here, the object both guarantees and refreshes the power of the knower, but any status as **agent** *in the productions of knowledge must be denied the object.*

—Donna Haraway

I.

MOUSE

One's fist would not fit inside its body. If one tried, the knuckles would snap the little folded clasp of the rib cage. It would leave no space for the glistening purses of organs. It might, in the nestle between knuckles, leave enough space for the heart, on average the size of an unripe bean, so pungently red it is difficult to understand its shape. It pumps one and a half milliliters of blood. But should you puncture the aorta with a needle (first manage to find it folded in the damp book of tissue), you could only draw two-thirds of that. Even then, the force exerted by your index finger and thumb creates enough tension on the arms and legs that they ball. Only the tendons, ligaments and bones, embedded like shards of a crushed porcelain spoon, prevent a complete erasure of form. Thus for this operation each of its four paws is pinned back (one, perhaps, for each cardinal direction). The blood is of equal thickness as our blood. The brain, which on the other hand is much smaller and resembles impure marble, can be retrieved without damage. The slender bridge of the hindskull is nipped and the immaculate ovalline lid lifted and discarded. As with us, the brain of an infant mouse requires less oxygen to survive, due to a thicker constitution of its blood.

When I enter the room. They know, as I enter and move the air and the air moves to them, if I took my route with hurry, if I had eaten before this, if I had made love before this, if I prefer perfume, if I prefer scented or unscented soap, if I never wash, if I had just come from the airplane or the subway station some blocks away, if I had walked under low-branched trees, if I had walked on the grass, if I had walked past the lilacs that are dying from blight, those lilacs planted on the walk between here and the room, the leaves frosted, clenched, even when it is nearly spring, when it is already spring and it is not cold. They may recognize me. I come often. It is preferred that one minimizes scent during a visit. They are in cages made of clear plastic. Cages are organized onto shelves. Shelves are arranged in walls. Walls curl around in an effort to conserve room. The room's light is red so as not to disturb. They rustle. Are limited to five per cage. Are identified within each cage with a simple numbering system. It is almost primitive. It need only reach five because there are no more than five per cage. The punch to identify them with can be used to pierce other materials, such as paper. The region of their ear needs to be distal enough that only skin (and not blood vessels) is incised. The numbering is almost stupid. Right. Left. Both. No ear piercings. Two on one side. Right and left are difficult. One must decide whether to orient so that one faces them, faces the black beads of their eyes, the red beads of their eyes, the downward look of their eyes, the looking away of their faces. Or the other choice (which is my choice) to hold them facing away with two fingers at their neck, while reaching down with the metal implement, aligning it with the body, and clipping out a part of the cupped ear.

One needs to sterilize the scissors beforehand, and the tweezers with ridged ends, the tweezers without teeth, the metal surfaces of the biosafety cabinet, the glass, the gauze still in its cotton-candy roll. The body needs cutting open and the skin to be parted and pulled back, the drape of fat shifted aside, the gauze used to wipe off the oil that seems to permeate the entire inside of the animal, that will glisten on the tips of the instruments. These are all equivalently important tasks. But the sterilization needs to be done before the anesthesia. The sterilization needs to be done an hour in advance because the most reliable method requires temperature and significant duration. Once the animal is anesthetized, speed becomes critical. We must orchestrate the entire process: the gas tanks needing to be purchased, the scissors needing to be brought, the surfaces needing to be cleaned, the body needing to be opened, the looking needing to be cast inside. This especially is our task: to want to see. What do we see? What do we bring when we see? We superimpose what we have seen to what we see now, which forces differences to be stenciled in, like a subtraction in a puppet show. That is a result. It becomes an art to learn how to tease it out. How to limn the fat thread of the artery from its red. How to lift it without losing opportunity, to know what pressure to apply with the ends of the instruments. To cause no noticeable damage.

The five of them in the cage are in theory identical. Differences arise with cohabitation. One becomes the dominant female, which can be distinguished by her greater size and weight. One becomes the runt. Awake, they sample the environment with scurries that take them back and forth across the surface of and interior of the bedding, which is composed of wood chips and little bouquets of fur, mixed with the compact punctuation of their feces. It is difficult to distinguish their characteristics while they are in motion; we need them to be still.

The animals are chosen at random for the procedure. The selection process becomes a kind of suspension, wherein the hand reaches in and the mind attempts to stay above the mouth of the cage, undiscerning, undiscriminating. For this procedure, we inject cells behind the eyeball. Specifically, we inject *hematopoietic cells* into the *retro-bulbar space* behind the wet globe of the eye, which enables cells to enter the bloodstream and home to where they desire. Home is a beautiful word, perfectly matched in its use as adjective and as verb. One by one, the cells follow the signals in the body they have entered, guiding them to the inner lining of periosteal bone, where, by chance finding a chamber it can use as abode, one might grasp the vessel wall in the marrow, and push like light through a half-open curtain.

BIRD

What is a bird? How much does it cost? How much does its cage cost? The going price for laboratory mice is twenty six dollars an animal. What is it for birds? They used to sell them around the river, dry wicker cages, dried ribs like parallel construction. They sold them before I was born. How much did one cost then? How much would it cost not to be silent? You do not speak for yourself. Not while doing science. Abandon the project. Go back. Go into the cage. Write about what you know. Tell me how to lower my voice near enough to silence so that the whole world can be heard, even the windings inside of this body can be heard, and finally I will know what stepped onto the park grounds and makes an about face, turns around to look.

It turns out we know nothing about birds, neither the birds that have returned to the ponds, nor the ponds themselves, artificial as slaughter, whose overgrowing weeds are pulled out each night and burned. (Who does the burning? Where do they put the ashes?) Late night, walking home by the re-growing, re-heightening reeds slender as the knife tracks on a butcher's board, I saw one bird hop branch to branch, like all of its kind baring a fantastically large breast, a rust red quarrel with air. I stopped. I looked.

I was innocent. I did not know what contamination looked like.
I did not know what it meant to be aseptic or to be sterile. I did
not know the ideal concentration of alcohol for causing death of
exposed cells. I did not know how much pressure to apply to the
mouse's front paws when taping them down so that they would
not break but would not come free. A mouse with an injury like
that would require euthanasia under protocol. And the
experiment would suffer a loss. And we may not see a result.

I did not know how to pull at the skin of the belly so that it
tightened up enough a needle could slide in as easily as sex.
There are prescriptions on how tightly to grip the animal. The
protocols get more detailed every year. They are overseen and
approved by a body becoming more exacting due to the
accumulation of animal welfare lobbyists in the government.
Accumulating like the sheer amplitude of knowing. There was a
time when I did not know what a mouse all alone looked like,
which was

that of something shivering so delicately it needed looking at
long and hard to even notice that it was reacting to being forcibly
isolated. What they said about mice was correct, and this one
would go insane if left alone too long, would paw in circles and
never stop. Their paws are slenderly proportioned. Their bodies
quiver. They only relax, completely relax, in the brief period
after death but before cooling. When did I learn legitimate
desire upon a recumbent body?

The mouths are parted at death. The teeth are long and narrow.
The eyes, black and moist, are prone to drying out when the face
stops and blinking ceases. In the eye pressed downwards, if the

mouse dies on its side, fluid pressure from the skull keeps the surface moisturized. But the eye that is pointed upwards dries out. The change starts at the center of the surface as a pinpoint of white that gradually spreads into the corners of fur, as if death were a drop of milk.

EUTHANASIA

The first thing it does
Is do a full backflip
Does the acrobatic mouse
Which rapidly explores
The perimeter comes back
To where it started
To where it sensed
What makes its ribcage
Slope-shaped as when
Thumb touches fingertips
And shudders as if
The hand attempting
Breaking open the palm
And the mouse's littermates
Put in the other room
And the pressurized gas
Put next to the airtight
Plastic cage
The shudders come more
Slowly and it looks
Over but backflips
The acrobatic mouse does
Before it stops blinking
I have been breathing

It stops blinking
Has not stopped breathing
Breathing is automatic
For the acrobatic mouse
The automatic routine
Undiscovered until now

When abundance of wrong air
Triggers spasms of clenching
I did not know I knew this
Final routine last encore
Possessed all along
This serious circus
Invented as it prays
Along the airtight seal
Not finding air not finding air
When I learned to swim
The feeling of too much water
The mouse in air like water
That is absolutely clear
Hay smell and excrement
Constant Nutrition and damp

In the cage of safety
In the cage of incipience
In the cage of experimental
Outcomes and saving
Your life with knowledge
Green chlorinated water I could
Shout could be heard belonged
To this side and now I come
To this side of the cage
My acrobatic mouse
Has finished its routine
Clawed feet won't click
The sole sound of this process was
Rapid clicks on the walls
Backflip and drown
The cage plastic smooth
No purchase to cling to

FOLLOW

The protocol
Go downstairs
Don't come back
Without the shaver
Then shave
The mouse
White hair on skin
Black hair on skin
Pale pink skin
Bathe it
Disinfect it
With astringent
Pinch the skin
Lift the mouse
Tent the mouse
Tent the skin
Slip the blade
Cut through
Underneath it
Use your hands
Fingers to firm it
Go up the back
To the neck
Head junction
Peel back it
Turn it over
Pinch the skin
Lift the mouse
Slip blade
Into underneath
Use your hands

Use your fingers
Fingers peel back
There to the white
Sacs on the skin
Flaps fold back
Pinch the tissue
Lift the mouse
Puncture the part
Pull as you cut
Tear the tissue
Off and mince
Mix with proteins
That reduce
The tissue into
Discrete cells
Decant into wells
Decant into plates
They are growing
There opening
And forgetting
The coarse thing
They were cut from

Here by the dirty river where people have come from, a silt and slime sliver as still as a gaze, birds have returned, and from ponds, the bodies of overgrown weeds are pulled out and burned. It is an artificial landscape, an artificial water, stones not to believe in, air for the slaughter, but even here, the torn net of bird chirps has closed again, around and now over an artifice. Birds, birdsong have returned, and from the ponds, those bonds between water and not enough death, the browning screens of weeds are pulled out, burned.

Ribbon of throat, maggot of air, singer of an outsized song that serves to find you a mate, whether pride is in your song or coquetry, I'll accept it: but can you sing into yourself, winding into the snail shell of your ventricular heart after the ants have reached the deepest coil, and past that, past that aperture, germs clean to a wick white, immune to sunlight until broken open? Isn't that what this muttering wants, to break open? Because plain day can never stop being a thing we can undo. All these rules set down without an arbiter, and us dazed as the body broken open into song, broken into fact and organ, omentum and meat. So what does singing do, this kind of song?

JOB

The body
Being carried into
The room inside
The white paper box
The same model used for cheap
Takeout with friends roommates
Cheap folded haphazardly
And sunlight falling in
For the first time
Photons shed
In radiative exhaust
Billowing into
The small lightweight
Too-heavy-to-be-a-bird's
Body patches on its back
Torn-off arcs flayed
Meanwhile this one
Still has a bit of wood
Bedding in its half-
Shut mouth

Meanwhile my scissors
My eyes look in at
Neat curl of organs
Light reflecting
The revealed insides
Of one whose mouth
Still clenches a
Wood cigar
Whose eyes still squint
Whose opened carnation-pink ribs

Arch over a mute
Heavy-lipped liver
Two ear-shaped kidneys
Spleen like an eyebrow
Intestines curled as a
Whorled homunculus
Omentum and muscle had
Pursed and kept underneath
Caressed in the sealed sheath
Hulled shut back then
Wet with light now
With the sight that
Slips sibilant in

II.

On the Mechanical Properties of Frozen Flesh

Because flesh is tensile   because—
because it has not yet gotten   cold enough
to diamond, to choose   a form
for the bitter, brittle   fracture that would come
with a touch; because   in fact
body freezes   even without cold, could
harden from organic solvents   that leach,
leave no trace, no yearning   for the event—
amethyst, pearl   dropped amber and
emeralds from the corners of the gall,   this
is the corpse broken into jewels   brief
gorgeous frieze: some pieces   glow because the body was
a clamorous show   in a lugubrious dead-end career
of intimate gestures   languorous turns
a flesh lingerie   for the dull tense soul to doff
that yet still thumps   on taut linen, a verse
of skin, nerve, never   slowing, only stops
in a permanent field of gems   jonquil lymph, a
histology of desire   to have been—
frozen gems that glide   across linoleum, dropped,
scatter, ride   their own hissing sublimation
into heaven's   indifferent reward.

DISSECTION

Bodice the color of rose. Ligaments
of cream. Undone; parted. Opening
and for a brief moment hooking breath
to a forced, indrawn stillness so as not
disturb whatever hypothesis might arise,
nor disturb the forceped hand that enters
with its set of impersonal instruments
as formal as *beauty*.

Let us observe now, and only observe
the dead eye turning white from a spot
least protected, of fullest exposure.
Beginning at the center of the eye, white
grows towards the lidded edge of fur
as the sclera dries.
What a delight to observe this:
the law of air in impersonal dryness

opening with Renaissance balance
on the glisten of fast-cooling meat;
how dryly it delights me,
an impersonal cool, and a cruel law
unfastening on the dead eye's surface;
how it delights me, possesses me,
to observe this complicated, supine thing,
and makes me thrill with detached arousal,
a theorem, a disease.

Opening now again, now another,
now as the doors systematically open
and close, and the freezer's white door

closes on opened bodies, bodies whose
eyes are shot through with white,
and the black branches outside are
the tendoned seams of many eyes,
and the black eye beneath me opens
to my unnecessary desire to see,
showing its cold white secret,
opaque in answer, widening,
as impersonal as I demanded it, all
that was desired to know, the white
dot in the eye that leads inside, in-
to the white noise of flesh,
while I, poised to better observe,
use this forceped hand to hold it open,
my body an impersonal instrument
that looks since it can, and is allowed.

Electron Microscopy of a Blood Smear

Delicate still, withholding still
in the false-colored images
(visibility the first deceit),

photographed from many angles
with strands of clot like a swimsuit
on coy burnt skin,

a flash fossil,
illuminated dot, soot-shaped grain,
Lot's salt wife in a field

evaporated to a hide
on the wide silica desert:
the dried-out leukocyte

baffled deformation
by drinking solvent,
ninety, one hundred percent

until formal, scorned the water
that clung to its flesh
and sluiced from the smear.

PERFUSION AND FIXATION OF THE LUNGS

Wet, peaked fur bunch   parted skin and ligament.

Pink anemones under   cliffs of stained snow.

Raw breath had once   drawn these pleural sacs, been drawn.

Fur-flap-color, dirt's color   ribs over an eager melt

that runs on and   seems cleansing because

clear. The tracheal insert is the new   beginning.

Dying collapsed these lungs, but needles   push fixative

into lobes that leak April   over a carcass

smelling of nothing that grows.   The clear bleed

plumps open alveoli,   formaldehyde that draws tight

adjacent amines (any two   will do) and hunger for

resemblance to the lived thing   replaces the older one

from the earliest suck   of pupped air and estuary.

SUBJECT

1.

They had us call them *patients*. The word is similar to *impatiens*, missing only the delicate four lobes that bruise more easily than even flesh.

I hold one mid-air—the usual grip, close to the spine to prevent defleshing of the tail's tip—and regard it. A name comes. My own name. My lover's name. My mother's. I am accidentally naming this *patient*. Why would I want that? I push the words back into my own breathing, or the basement breathing through vents and ducts

but the name holds. In my hand, it looks untouched. Like the ruins of a culture. *Where even the birds do not know to be scared of humans.*

When I handle them, I notice their differences. They are of course individuals. I see their entire body at once—sleek, black fur, bulbous eyes, vibrating whiskers. They peer over the plastic cage walls to smell the air beyond the transparent siding.

I am in a hurry and they disobey. They dart under the bedding when I lift the lid to their cage, a shoebox-sized enclosure of torn cotton and excrement. But I always find them. We designed the bedding not to hide them. And they forget to tuck in their tails. Their tail leads into the body, joins and thickens to the spine, the vertebrae, and up to their sleek forward skulls.

The only trespass is to waste. They are a resource. To destroy them without appropriate usage would be wasteful. To allay them by attaching unnecessary anthropomorphic sentiments would also be wasteful, because it would squander my intellectual capital. *Be not afraid*.

2.

My actions are approved.

My actions as verbs. Feed. Hoist. Do not dangle. Place inside cage but do not drop. Number. But not name. Check. Stroke. Euthanize. Be watchful. Remove from cage. Open. Do not perform secondary euthanasia if major organs are removed. Realize that there is no wrong,

that it is for my use

and later I walk down the halls

with a ziplock bag in hand

that I do not look at. I look

outside. At the light that comes in.

It was the light outside

that guided us here, wasn't it?

And in my other hand, I hold

what I came for.

Black eye beginning to pale
from the center, turning white
delicately towards the edge of fur.

Black eye beginning to pale
when the law of air descends
and dries glistening from meat.

Black eye beginning to pale
in a feint. This one, anesthetized,
had forgotten to blink.

Black eye beginning to pale.
Bodies curl around stiff faces
behind the freezer's marble door.

Black eye beginning to pale.
The bird outside has no qualms shrieking.
What did it learn last night?

Black eye beginning to pale.
The sternum snipped and pulled
back and taut, a paper fan.

Black eye beginning to pale,
a heart beating in the dead thing,
and other wonders of the world.

Black eye beginning to pale
in the freezer of wonders. Exiting
with empty hands again.

Black eye beginning to pale.
Is there any red like the thick red
of the spleen, iron and soft?

Black eye beginning to pale.
There is no shape like the liver,
neither leaves nor a cupped hand.

Black eye beginning to pale
in this deconstructed body.
Spread, catalogued, informative.

Black eye beginning to pale.
Doors slide open and close easily.
My haunches move me easily.

Black eye beginning to pale.
Bioengineered eyes
stare back from the future.

Black eye beginning to pale.
So sings Orpheus's severed head.
Instead of singing I open.

Black eye beginning to pale
for the law of air descends.
Ribs spread out like a paper fan.

Halogen lights are shining outside.
A heart beating in the dead thing.
Black eye beginning to pale.

MUSE:

I practice my smile in the mirror   chordate that I am.
I hear a vehicle engine   pulling in on the driveway.
How can I be in this climate   a mammal at all?
Orcas drown a whale calf   and eat the tongue
no more. I am more of a flower   I eat only sun
my skin the horny green   of a peony's hide:
my calyx mounts with bone   my stamen stands on stilts
a pistil sweets exudate   pale corolla waits to wilt.
Do you doubt my nature?   I bring out of my side
a skeletal vase   pulling water up freshets
in crinkled xylems   plumped petals for a face:
my current face wanders   on cartilaginous bone
balancing point for the head   and new blood's source
while old blood breaks   in the spleen's charnel house.
I stare with discovery   at this tongue-shaped face.
O flower, wait for the ants   to carve up your face.

Dead Thing

Some part of you put inside it with the bodies
The freezer in the hall emptying every other day
The huge duty of it, endlessly hungry
When you do not find it you empty

The freezer in the hall emptying every other day
Some part of you put inside with the bodies
The huge duty of it, endlessly hungry
So open me now again

What is it that you are looking for this time
The freezer in the hall emptying every other day
So open me now again
With that old unfrightened desire

What is it that you are looking for this time
The kidney and liver carmine still
With that old unfrightened desire
Kumquat heart, tooth shaped lung

The kidney and liver carmine still
The young jump for life, the sick die fast
Kumquat heart, tooth shaped lung
Some part of you is endlessly hungry

The young jump for life, the sick die fast
Some part of you put inside with the bodies
Some part of you is endlessly hungry
When you do not find it empty

Cervical Dislocation of Mouse

It would be finished in the next moments.
But those moments seem almost infinite.
One reaches for the time after the finish
for that expected hour, that unreal future
to be real, when the intervening breaths
had been completed. And so it is after

those minutes and those hours: the after-
wards, so reached for over moments
counted and completed breath by breath,
had made the present allow the infinite.
We are both here, in body, in the future
after what would happen had finished.

Time moves with such smooth finish,
it is often the other way around. After
the sun has set, it is suddenly the future.
The clattering down the street. Moments
later it passes us like normal, with finite
duration, a moment held in, a breath.

Some materials last without breath.
That plastic scalpel there. The cut finished,
wounds leaving a residue of finite
spit. Its structure consists of one after
another of styrene monomer, with moments
of freedom congealed from shifting further.

An inert backbone binds the future.
Airtight and does not live or breathe.
Soft enough that the moment
teeth sink in a bite, it will lose its finish
and turn white and opaque. And after
it is disposed of continues a finite

duration, which (to us) seems as infinite
as a moment on the cusp of its own future...
The one held down, the other, after
donning gloves, allows finite breathing
by the one beneath, until both finish.
Both waiting for the momentary

flinch to pass. And in the moment
afterward, the finite acquires a finish
and a future with no need for breath.

Organelle Isolation from Whole Blood

Its back a tensed hum
anticipating my cut

into it, by which I take a thimble-
ful of blood,

blood that will return—
seeping out—

in a week's time
from springs in bone.

There is one such bone
in front of our chest

where a hand claps
to declare a *me*:

promontories,
breeding grounds

for flocks of erythrocytes
with pricked-out nuclei

to replenish
what curdles in spleen.

I delete them using
ammonium chloride buffer

to purify the lymph-
ocytes, leukocytes,

pale white with
a citrine touch,

the rare subset.
The speed is set

to drag a blur
down to the center

until pales break:
the inner parts

with denser ore
bruise out

for the glass needle
to gather and

extract: purest
strip, from every

body freed.

                      requires a gram
of discarded gristle   stammering
impenetrant light   congealed tooth
useless until   untangled, trans-
sected by a blade   and immured to glass,
to lacerate   and interpret with
a thousand cuts

                   into vibrancies
carefully laid, more   petal than page,
in an epilogue of glass   no phrase
needing translation   each bared
each denuded   of coy
opacity, prepared   for the lens
in the curtained room   dark as the heart
in an intact chest. There

                 the body
is peal   seduced to particle,
the hidden visible   buried bright
abraded of the tangible   or just thinned
in slice after slice   of enforced visibility:
each cut goes deeper   into the secret gram,
towards, past   the center of mass,
details collate

               a map that
constitutive sight   bleeds in, trans-
forms what had been   mere meat,
blasts a mass scrap   into imaged fact,
imaginable, exposited   onto the screen,
a gristle bit   phlegm-like lode
blueprint truth.

SHUT

Two-week time point. Still life snapshot
slide from the limb. We had implanted
coated metal into bone. We wanted to see

what would happen. Part of bone always dead
but malleable. From that streaks
tangy protein, visible there, the edges of fire,

blue halo where cells and their living carbon begin,
flanged like a tongue towards, almost into
but merely against the fragment of foreign

ore, the metal prepared, engineered
to seduce, to persuade the abruptly still
body, using a painted-on dowry

of bone morphogenetic protein two
and platelet derived growth factor.
The bone persuaded to grow.

Meanwhile the seam
flanges with Coomassie's blue, with
digited exultation, as if it cannot bring

metal close enough to periosteum's skin.
The seduced always says yes.
Thick white-to-blue

clouds of mineralizing strata,
the Safranin's red, hemotoxylin.
The body blooms. Incessant ravishing.

III.

1.

The knowledge we gathered is no longer useful.

The system you understand shifts and makes no sense.

And this is the body you spent years getting used to.

Tomorrow, the light will not recognize it.

Light has no language for what is smaller than a hairpin turn of a
    chromatin.

Light must be choked in order to name the smaller things.

My name could change.

We shall say what we shall say and call it knowledge.

I learned this language to subsist and to compass between myself
and the unknown.

I should not have learned it.

I should have been a fish in a world of rising water

boring in with immense color until it seems that it was never knowledge
that was gained from the set of things as they are, having been now
turned-away-from by the world

and yet still a knowledge.

A trust that can't be turned from.

Trust in the thing that is an inhabitance of it.

Of the only thing I am standing on and not

just the dirt slitted with plant roots and leaf-stains made up of mashed chlorophyll pigments, drying up now, pregnant with incidental light and nothing to pass it on to

here in the stomach of the beast

punched open to the ceiling lights.

2.

They have invented poems with algorithms.

They can be done with objectivity.

They work by concatenating locally intelligible
phrases and improve by introducing a theme
known but not spoken of. That

is how they work.

There is a chance it won't work.

They have a name for infrequent events: it was
worked out by examining the number of Prussians
who were kicked to death by their horses.

The man who discovered this had a name that means *fish*.

I pick up the first thing at hand at this table,
the first thing with words, it was a postcard
on which someone had written *Thank you*

Fish feel pain as I feel pain but fish do not hurt.

Their pain is written in the asymmetry of missing scales,
the operculum that covers the richly vascularized gills
lifted on one side and cannot go back down.

The fish feels terror, which is the response to fear

fear blanks into terror   The mean and the variance

fearless fish lidless sleek   are the same value.

The scar formation process is the same between
human and fish.

The scar is a result of the deposition of an aligned
matrix where the matrix had been random because
closure needs to be fast to stop the emergence
as though the body fears the thing that has left.

3.

Before I get to the two trees.

Because I do not know what one is.

What one of anything is.

Though I know the difference between the infinity of reals
and the infinity of counting numbers
and I have counted excellently.

Though with my eyes I have disentangled the tangling branches
of the trees, seen through the window (still bare,
their buds right now invisible from such a distance)

before I get to the two.

This one tree.

Whose definition includes the water (half the mass is water)
exiting like a soul from the organic body.

So shrugs that inorganic water.

And yet is included in this [tree], in this set, counted in it.

As is this knotted carbon fixed from air for a duration.

As is—briefer—the small heat of the tree, which my own hot hand
    cannot feel.

My hand put against the bark, the material of my palm

and the thing about this hand such that I do not lose it

to the bark, to the coolness, to the tree, to the incomplete definitions
    of the world.

It must be human to accept

that this is *a* tree (right now: *the* tree) despite the minglings
that we know occur, that we recite, that we recite

in the same way that the traversal of these disparate sounds
and silences does not loosen

in the manner of a fraying cloth.

Is that the wrong assumption.

Lineaments in apparent solidity and the inferences of composition,
as from the way salt burns.

Having stood before the definite and in seeing made myself lonelier:
the faultiness inherent of our most basic assumptions
of the individuality of things and of counting

the definite mercy of closed forms

which cannot be taken off by the living body.

4.

I can number the days before earthworms emerge

and I can number the robins that live in this neighborhood

fattening on the earthworms, that eat dirt for sand

and with the same mouth they sing

and the trees sing too, if one could hear them

for they are all mouth and their roots hunger at water,

for their bodies are entirely covered with tiny mouths that let out

threading whispers of water and they would die if they did not sing
    that way

and what could you ask of such a thing?

5.

That cannot shut their mouths

that exhale water in the day

that breathe in moisture at night

that are called the weep holes in brick.

Hole in the wall to let out weep water.

To go through the facing wall.

We had to use up this much, use it all up.

And lapsed back?

How much of this life already lived?

How much of the earth's spin already lost?

One cannot respect the landscape.

Not even in the cold winter.

The brick crumbs, the mortar salt.

Be still in this landscape.

Still is a form of movement.

Being so still I hold onto my breath.

And my thousand metabolic fires still going.

This is the apparatus.

6.

Remove confounding factors (contamination).

Test something that is certain to work.

Test something that is certain not to work.

The unknown, now: test it.

Again remove confounding factors (contamination).

Repeat the test.

(Tell me what counts as contamination.
Does it include my subjectivity, which I must tease from
the *hunch* of what to look for, should I look

forward to when I am strictly unnecessary?)

Spray antiseptic again to undo
the thin lipid membrane, undo the boundary,

cross the erased line to undo proteins within, that are being
turned in-
ward by reorienting the charged amino acids, huddle them

to create a kind of amnesia
on the smooth metal, the smooth glass surface.

I spray it on my hands when I enter to learn.

My hands go in. A cleverness goes in. A germ.

7.

Thump thump of an indrawn

Accreting disc

Withdrawing from

Mere resemblances

Shadow addition

Shadows, scaled like

Bulbs and all

Budding building

Knowledge is this

Pare off this and that

The intentless dither

Whereby the cure

The root into your body

(Which you do not regard)

(As an intimacy yet)

Becomes known—

Contralto tearing

Of flesh, the scissors

Trimming open the body

Trimming open *my* body

Alloy of flesh, my ears acknowledging

The sound of body neatly torn

As if somewhere else

It was not personal

No malevolent planet

Purely body, pure paucity

Puissant drone of intent

Intent of merely being

(Flare of reflected)

(Enunciations)

8.

That which is given but cannot be owned:

a piece of knowledge, existing there,

a body warmed on a rock. That

this hand, for example, knows how to grasp how to release

how to release potassium ions which will stop the heart if

crushed for more than a few minutes. A part

of the body. They say that a body once swallowed the universe

in its throat. Is it still there? How it seems, everything with the attempt

to be in understanding of it, seems an attempt

to love the body that I wish

laughingly wish I could

sometimes put my hand into

just to learn. I am still waiting to find out

how the body can remain closed after so much effort,

the fact of it just apprehended in the effort of loving,

but this is what I meant to tell you

that the universe is still there behind the tongue

the secrets are all there

prenable because, under a light microscope,

I can see the body containing them

its skin voluptuously holding it all intact

and the darker nucleus where they sleep

dark enough and solid

so where is the button to press

to get the chromosomes to untangle

to stopper time and grow the fruit

where all knowing is fixed

9.

Dying is no longer incumbent on the heart.

The heart's role in this determination has been handed to the brain.

The brain's cessation involves the neurons.

The neurons fragment into a mere approximation.

A mere approximation of the living body is the dead body.

The dead body approximates the living thing we remember.

Remember learning about linear approximation?

Linear approximation to solve the intractable?

The intractable will now be solved by machines.

Machined replicas of our dreams will come in bubble-wrapped sheaths.

Sheaths of myelin wrap our central neurons in soft clouds.

Clouds of images I recall: the Charles River, real clouds.

Clouds fogging up what I actually remember.

What can I actually remember? Of my own face, for example.

Exemplary memory of mask-of-skin over bones,

bones plated over a forgetful pinecone of nerves searching,

searching the face that the eye slowly examines.

The eye slowly examines each quadrant of the thing.

The thing in the mirror is recognized as a familiar face.

A familiar face, then eyes close and the memory starts dying.

10.

In the end, the body could believe in little.

It believes in the cud that makes itself go forth.

It believes that time is dependable.

It believes that time does not expand depending on how fast the
   body goes,

that the time it is planning to take

is precisely how much time the world takes.

I freeze down the cells when I want more time.

In the cold, molecules take longer to become overripe.

The rush of ions shimmer like stray thoughts

on the edge of a hardening cusp, as if

their movements were close to light speed

and time seems to dilate. Imagine a dream

of glassy water which does not ice,

preserving the membrane that would puncture

like a pronunciation at the tip of the soft palate

while the world around loosens from motion

into an innocent stillness.

But it is not complete. Something still ticks.

When I stand up, it will take

the heart nearly three beats

to pump blood back to the brain.

At the window, watching a flower bloom for the entire afternoon.

The magnolia by the window takes five days to go from bud (hairy,

slightly engorged) to full flower. Blooming at a rate

thousands of breaths long. It is a matter of distribution. If you

added together the force of each kiss that brushed your forehead

and applied that within the space of a millisecond, a micro-

second, it would punch through your skull. They say that one can
    slow light down

by shining it through a heavy species of glass. It does not slow down
    at all.

Within glass, from atom to atom, as though from room to room

it moves with the same speed

shedding as it goes, as it must, until

presented to the open

for the next purchase

11.

Matter is ongoing   in widening distances.

The yellowed grasses bunched on the edge of the road now creep
a little in between the asphalt which was planted on bedded earth,
dumped on older grass, which itself had been new on an older continent

and the animal too

in ambiguous preparation: one foot

placed after the other.

If a body, having entered the earth, having had the earth cover it

sinks tectonically and reaches the stratum to produce pressures high
enough that temperatures are raised to the point where water
    would boil,
it will become purified into pitch

which is the same material that makes this straight line

bisecting a plane by which stand low shrubby trees, or one tree

that has dropped fruit onto the tarmac,

the recent shattered one whose imprint of cored water already
    dried up

(dehydration also the first step for the formation of tar)

but the sweetness still there

on the asphalt

in the same way that the word *bitumen* seems to have *blood* in it,

the bitumen in the straight line that goes

toward a sky white

with untarnished scope.

IV.

SEMELE AND DIONYSUS, AS INDUCED PLURIPOTENT STEM CELL

It was not like the red poppy,   whose lids leaned towards
detachment from too much shudder   of rain, flaying from
the hurt point. It was more like   mud. Her speech developed
a lisp. This because her teeth moved from the death of cells
that would have anchored them in place. Throughout her body
there was death and decay—that was normal—
but without replacement. The cells for replacement
had been damaged and so had to be sloughed, meaning she
had to be sloughed. Even the parts of her that were not
meant for growth, like the cells of the heart, which had been there
since girlhood, could not be sustained. In the end it was mud,
mud melting through a slender cage of snow. Her brain was damaged.
There was not much left of her before the end.

The godlike part of her, a pluripotent cell resistant
to radiation, had been transplanted under the skin
of a host and called her son. He was then like a breath
not yet skimmed up from the organs hugging laterally
the sternum, those two sponges shaped like lobes
of a broken orange. He was the oath that had yet
to be stapled into the inhalation. There had been
no utterance yet: he was a term of water
crouched on a mountain whose proof would be
the muddy terminus of germ-layers and differentiation,
necessary for him to become what he was to become: a god.
But the water under the skin was wrong. There was no way
the thing would grow into the mirror of that expectancy.
The sealment is too tight. What kind of space

is a thigh for that. When he steps out he is nothing that is
expected, but the parts are there. All the parts are there.

The rows of teeth are there. He had been broken like a reflection
that a pebble had plunked into and put back together.
He was the reimagined light melted from its shards into literal trash
because he was trapped, godlike, in disarrangement: a teratoma.
And the momentum of his displacement seemed to tilt
the forest so that he was leaning into the turgid puddles
of the floor paned up to meet him. The birds greeting him.

The ravens darker than fragmented leaves greeting him,
leaves from the season before and the season before that,
from when there had been enough light to cut each feather, glide
        along on
the oil spumed from preening. The oxbirds open their mouths. Each
        one becomes
an open flower that cannot bloom hard enough
and there is a slit   in the upper part of each mouth
he could not remember   but seems to mean
he is delicious, dismembered   as he had been whole
in that indivisible finger-sized dark: mulberry.

He proceeded as if he were not a rearrangement
and reportioning of what was not new, an extra tooth
from too much exposure, squeezed up through gum,
but was wholly new, and the world needed him
because the world was what he could feel
at the sense of what he was, there at the boundary
between what seemed inside him and what impinged,
the surface entire and thick and firm as his throat
which could not have enough of the summer odor,

which could not have enough of the sporing rain
fallen after a long preparation of fungal abscess,
the heart nearly choked in its support of red broadleaves,
those clenched trees that were so still, and each

still a stage in preparation for his arrival:
black staghorn branches slitting with bud, their
venation the most efficient cut of air. And then the deep
consistent ring that the earth makes. And then the thin
fragments, the unleavened flakes of quarried mud.

ARGUS DREAMS OF APPLES

Argus's whole body leaks with apertures
like the orb of a blue-bottle.

He looks at what he sees. A cow
and apples a number of fields over, invisible
but full of apparent surfaces, that he describes
as though he knows them in the way
he imagines that he knows them,
their topography and those surfaces
knotting to the axis where surface itself puckers
and disappears. He imagines apples breaking

into even more surfaces, each clean as
the white wall behind a butcher's window.
The apples make him feel alone
deep in his mind. And the leashed cow lows.

Argus knows, with arctic intelligence, that his eyes
in their argyle arrangement, will be sealed
into lines. At the current moment, his skin crawls
with eyes; he uses them to see himself sometimes,
and he is almost full of visions of Argus

as he is of the apples surrounded by nymphs
of that other story, nymphs dancing during
the watch they keep. He watches them too:
the panorama aches.

How unreluctant he would be for the god
that is bound to come to escort him away
by unhooking the panel of vision from him

as though it were simply a slide through which
light could shine, illuminate what he saw.

He once saw the nymphs tossing apples around
for the apples were nothing to them. One apple
broke against a tree into spiced, sharded flesh
and he watched it disclose its surfaces,
as wet and rough as sweat in a cow's hide.

ABATTOIR

ORACLE

What did it mean by the words *can you help him*?
They came to me from his mother via my mother
and I wore them like the unwashed shirt beneath
the lab coat, my body wearing them underground
into facilities where animals are kept.

DOUBLE

What did it mean by the words *can you help him*?
The words came to wear me. Like my unwashed shirt
wearing its lab coat. Both of them wearing my body
underground where animals are kept.

DISEASE

The fundamental question is always this:
what does it mean by *my body*? When
does the body stop becoming your own?
When does part of your body stop recognizing
how to stop ravening? When does it turn its face from you?

RECALL

In the body, blood shares its birth place with mineral.
Cancellous bone cathedrals. Trussed trabeculae.
They would have given him the bones from the broth
with anise seed and pork blood to suck, until he lost
strength to pull in air.

ANCESTRY

I met him only once even though we shared blood
and our mothers would pass whispers to each other
like leaves of the same tree. And that was when we had
a shared sparseness of black hair, a shared smooth face,
the same birth year.

BAD LUCK

We knew cancer was eating his bones because his bones
were replaced by a cheap knockoff material. That is how
his right arm broke. Cancer wears the body and hungers
and looks like the body and repeats it and lies.

APPROVED PROTOCOL

Did the words *can you help him* mean my face appearing
in the mirror and following me into the underground facility?
Many things wanted to wear my body underground
but my face, recognizably human, was the strangest of all.

IMMUNE

A *model organism* means there are bodies that are metaphors.
A mouse is an experimental metaphor for the human.
There are two things in a metaphor and one of them is imagined.
When I say, My body is a metaphor for intellectual curiosity,
which hungers like the body, my body stops being real.

EURYDICE

Take off your backpack and overcoat when you go down
and hang them on the rack or store them in the coded lockers.

Take off your scent and your careful maintenance of being human.
Take off your face except the eyes. None of these is necessary.

ORPHEUS

Remove your need and your hope for a cure. Have you finished
washing everything off from the world containing birdsong?
You will fail if they stay on your skin, like the scent rubbed
on you from another man's shirt.

WEAN

Hissing from the gas valve. The flow rate into the cage is read
from the ball that bobs on a tight invisible column,
quivering until the flow stops, and it drops, dead.
Unplug the tube and take off the plastic lid of the cage.
Nothing is cleaner than the smell of a freshly opened body.

HOME

In the failed treatment, the new blood wanders the body
in search of old familiarities, and pushes at
the seared vessels in bone like animals under ice pushing
for air. We inject blood into mice by inserting a needle
into the cupped space behind the eye.

FIREFLY

But there was so much to see. The spleen's rill redder,
the gall darker, and the whisper of the opened thing
louder than anything unopened. It muttered answers
of color and beauty. I whispered, *Can you help him*?
It replied: *Help him*.

ANTISEPTIC

Did the springs around Delphi cleanse the person or
their body? I could have pinched the beaded cuff
and peeled off the glove like a flayed hide, but I kept
my skin beneath the faucet's bite, cold like failure.

FIGURE

The ears punched with holes for enumeration. A chewed-
gum of brain. The pelvic bone like a sycamore seed planted
in the haunch, the whole unopened body weighing less
than a deck of cards. Small enough to shelter in my palm.

BONE

The careful washing out of marrow and debris. A thin
isthmus of the whole, gnawed and now excised,
held up to the ceiling lights. Its coarse spongy translucence
visible, looked at. How like a long-limbed bird's.

for Z L., 1988–2014

Returning from the opera, carrying the experience of having
watched the soprano's body tense in the mechanism of vocal
production, the diaphragm that had been trained rigorously
clamped there in the middle of her body and moving like an
immense tensed tongue (I pictured her body made of glass,
transparent, colorless, unimportant, and the diaphragm a stiff
red mist slowly unfolding at the center)

at the same place where I was making an incision that night in
the experimental subject (the mouse—we call them *subjects*) after I
had cut the loose skin at the base of the rib cage and after I had
cut up the sternum and retracted the scissors and made another
cut just beneath the ribcage and followed its contours down the
sides in an embrace: *that* was when I cut the diaphragm, after
which the ribs were pried open and the animal gently disrobed
and enlarged to the size of my palm, and the heavy cluster of
heart and lungs still sewn

to the ribs and dangling heavily like a scrotum and the heart
beating even as the ribs were separated from the knobbed seam
of the spine as if life were attempting to supersede its stopping
point (spurious: life is mechanical), for which the heart could
continue beating even after the cervical dislocation and the five
minutes of carbon dioxide euthanasia in the custom-designed
cage whose umbilical opening at the base lets in water to give life
and suffocating gas to give death to the body before it becomes as
bountiful as a field: Look at me now, it goes, look at how
apparently I resemble that depiction of dominion and power, *The
Great Red Dragon* of W. Blake

which has his secret flesh (though I am female, like all the other mice due to higher population densities being sustainable with my sex) turned to you who elected this. You recline like the Sun. You watched me, during the euthanasia, loosen my neck so that my head, extended backwards as far as it could above the invisible sea, drooped slowly, as if unknotting from its dumb hoard of instincts and devoid of intelligence (but I found the eyes in your face and held them as you watched me) in the languid smoothness of meat relaxing of its own accord, in a mechanically compassed arc, in a move that an actress would have made. Now you may say, with the humility of your ceiling lights and ventilation hood, your autoclaved scissors and narrow lamp, that you have thus obtained the right—which has surely become yours—to extract the qualities of truth and doubt (the latter a coil of razor wire) from my flesh. Take it from me, and say it does not cut open your hands.

AN EXPERIMENT OF MIND AND BODY

Holding my hand above my inner arm   a finger there
the contact tightens   but shakes   and cannot steady
my fingertip skin gotten rough from use   the other reacts as
though frightened but it is only still   mine and therefore
neatly presented to itself   this circuit that hardly involves
me when completed   lit and lived as a spark
in the brain   there at its base, throwing up the more

guttural notion of being   for if the spine were cut
then for a little while   the nerves would still send
marrows of hunger upwards   reminding reminding keep on
the metabolic song   of producing trash and devouring
that fare or else risk   forever stopping the mawed needing
because stopping is like that utility pole   you saw while driving
tall dark full of mass, you slam into it   and it slams back
with an equal momentum of approach   does it not seem infinite

I clutch my own approach   my arms embrace or garnish this mass
known so well   known so strangely: one's own self, how slight
to know what it feels like   what does it feel like   what does it feel
kneeling and the floor pressing the femur   bending the foot
into an unnatural angle   forcing the straight line into the body
which temporizes   the slow mossing of bone, for example,
or the pupils that expand   when circumscribed
by the larger dark   how much colder is the neutral chill

lunch's room temperature   that slides into   almost behind
     the face
the munching to slake appetite   the rutting glissando
lower teeth's grind and further grind   then the ruckus is swallowed
mash of wet matter   with air that is caught   and then the body

is sullen   how much harder do you need to pinch yourself   awake
do you need to be reminded by the bayleaf scent   of sunset
of birds   roosting into trees forever in the near distance

After Francis Bacon

Two eyes, one face   and one smacking gullet
parts of a toughness   that won't let
any flap go   without a force to unstrap, to rend ligature.
Sometimes now   I climb back
into this refrigerator   return to what
lies bored on its back   or when curled on its side
resembles bacon   and made up
from stirruped parts, stern   mayonnaise-
colored meats, tendons   rising like sticks
screwed   into bone, or rather
into the slick peel   coating the chalked bole, com-
posite with a name but who knows   wrapped round, cling-
                               wrapped knit
kaleidoscopic. This sole   honesty, old home
of soul's intelligence: each attempt to it
like a voice flung into echo   nothing to
persuade except the mind   that it is here in this at all
and all, this graveyard   hope, owned, won't
leave but will tender what   this quietus knows.

After a 28-Gauge Needle

The needle parts skin   nearly without violence.
The flesh moves around the bevel laminarly.
The beveled head contains no neurons but
it proceeds sensitively, with an unmatched delicacy
like the first proceedings of marital love,
or a posited theorem, so far un-executed.
Its medium is forged metal containing what could be imagined
as a gullet or a urethra:
intent had made its thin body a vacuum
and a hole, a hollow currently trapped
by the small gurgle of air.
The mind quickly enters the point.
It becomes a proboscis. The snout of an animal
entering a forest clearing, where disturbance
could be the end of its survival.
What matters is the terminal point at the bevel.
The bodies are described by a number
derived from the Stubs wire gauge system.
They range from the thirty-four–gauge needles
capable of being inserted into the eye
with little damage, to seven-gauge ones,
laughably thick: there is no fear
in them, their damage would be obvious.
A patent war was fought over the general design
and the question of the efficacy of what was
administered by this route.
The thin ones are wisps and the eye scrambles for
the tip, which cannot be quite made out without
effort, but caught, then, the termination of metal
into air: how quickly
it becomes almost an extension

that is controlled so finely
even the body's native appendages cannot compete
with its zeal.

THE SPEAR OF ACHILLES, AS GENE EDITING

Why leave the ash standing and swaying
on the Greek mountainside,
twigs tilting, tear-shaped leaves
shading and shading the slopes of Pelion
where Thetis wed Peleus before the gods
and partisans were shot?

And why let the code go on carrying
what it means by your father's forehead,
your mother's air, you river child,
to-be killer child, when an enzyme can
cut like the leaf-shaped iron tip
fastened there with a ring of gold?

Why not let it crack the bronze helmet
and cut into the bony skull
that had developed from a kind of memory,
cutting as a cough cuts a candle
at the designated nucleic acid sequence?
Why the wailing on city walls

while cutting down below fashions
perfected children, future children,
and why shouldn't each grin
of brilliant smile clean as steel wool,
spotlessly engineered, try to win
the race and the war, if it can?

So why not tumble down the great ash
not bothering to store the leaves in the warehouse,
prototypes that aren't of consequence,

and loop the tassel through the iron?
What does *nucleic* mean? And *son*?
What can it do but heal?

Poor soul, the center of my sinful earth,
an earth of metabolic flame, of blemished
and unblemished cells intent on giving birth
to still more cells, in scalloped rows, squished
whorls. How it seems we might dismember
each edge until we reach the body's center.
But with no edges, can there be a center?
Or a single dot, door no one can enter?
I reached it once in flesh preserved intact
from slow immersion in formaldehyde,
for I was willing to subtract and subtract
until I reached the spot where soul might hide.
Poor sinful earth, that I could not leave whole
because some poet claimed it held the soul.

During the wait from *being* to *have been*,
I pictured myself as part of that clean
lunge into the future, towards its windows.
The sun was high—too high to disappear—
when yesterday I went outside. I watched it send
white panels onto the suddenly clean
sidewalk, and I walked in the utter sense
that I would stay in this immortal theater;
I'd make it past the metal fence, the shrub,
beyond the experiment and its excuses
and the dead end, the abrupt little bulb
of asphalt meeting sidewalk and houses
and fenced-off land, which only shadows
could pass, shadows too thin to hold fear.

(I left the lab) (I walked across the
earth) (a city was built on it) (was made
from built-up sides of buildings) (the
sides had space between them) (I saw a glade
of space) (I turned into it) (watched it withdraw
each time I turned) (the streets made a city)
(its edge was made of railroads) (freeways) (I saw
a building) (it was made of holes) (a city
of entrances and exits) (bodies entering and
exiting) (and the bodies made from pieces)
(pieces made from timepieces) (contraband)
(poached) (but always) (like in a fleece
a broken fingernail) (in something caught)
(I am looking at it) (the body) (I have not

done a thing) (besides look) (at the body)
(and feel) (because isn't that what I am)
(contingency of knitted time) (city
to which each wound has been) (a tomb
broken) (but regarded as though) (under
anesthesia) (when only the dull ache)
(from nerves awakening) (in the border)
(tell) (how sad that the deadspaces lack
feeling) (and so the wounded flesh itself
feels nothing) (like nothing) (alas for the rite
of closure) (skin creeps like a sea-shelf
over a space that leaks) (the streetlight
leaks its own halogen) (a shadow runs
down the street) (oblique to all presence)

We are blasts that were born inside a body,
a dark pouch that was long ago and barely
remembered. Here on the surface plastic
you sowed us, you scattered us sparsely
and kept a flat emptiness between us.
But we do not remain where you spread us,
we travel and we stretch, we reach into
the liquid surrounding us to pluck each
fruit you provide and we divide. The truth
is that we always hunger. We have come
to put another square inch of this hard
surface hurting our mouths into our mouths.
We are that hungry for the darkness from
long ago, the birthplace inside the body.

There are five types of grass in this clearing.
The first type is virgin grass. The second
is young grass that pulls us into the clearing
deeper because our bodies are clear, fecund,
and there is so much tenderness to feel.
The third type of grass is mature grass:
we watch it shrink as our torsos congeal
steadily over it. The fourth, old grass,
has been stunted by our crowding because
we have covered the ground with our bodies
until grass cannot breathe and our bodies
crowd in. We have choked it, satisfied.
And the fifth grass type is grass that is dead.
We are the dead and they are growing over us.

BLAST

Reach confluence, reach
growth arrest, live and die
the two week span, detach,
erode and float free

as when we (another we) began
but after having already, at the haunch,
inside the haunch, begun, the beginning
which had to be released

with scissors and dispase into spheres,
spherical already but now individuated,
tendered from protein holds
and kept cold while cutting at

this compact white, this oily fiber,
molecularly twine-on-twine,
hydrophobic stubs, lysine-knotted-linked,
and after it looks torn

dump five thousand cells onto the plate,
each slitted bud constructing
amino acids into meat,
each uncurling in an hour

from an untethered ball
two tenths of hair's thickness
into ellipsoids whose hourly
cortical distensions bleed

their lower halves flat into ever-
sharpening lamellipodia
that grope for reach, for touch
being programmed

to maximize contact
with hardness and attachment,
to minutely repeat those stiff
clutched integrin holds, tearing

apart to let go of what had just tilled
blank plastic or seemed to,
tack back into actin in-
sides, cabled skeleton, cytosol

flowing about as restless
as insects in puddle-water,
because there is nothing godlier
than a clean appetite

for the next square inch, half-
inch lined up for observation,
apparent, senseless, but no use
stopping, gristle ungirdled and

dispersed onto the reflective
field of passive plastic permissive-
ness, crop of nodules, flotsam,
terminally differentiated local

craterings where excessive
matrix deposition strangulates
the living, the race is finished,
every cropped throat poisoned

and the next drove drifts down
to the plate (remember to feed)
(remember to change growth
media) (it is getting used up)

MACHINE LEARNING

This is the future form
of words that mirror
the processing of meat
material's wet flesh from
skin. Also called fleshing
of the meat from bone,

from body. This is that
cleanest hypothesis,
call it coldness,
it iterates repeatedly,
a lack of preference
broken scansion

so as not to be polluted,
the bones of pooled observation:
be undressed of any known
term (feelings, moral
wrong), into the new
form, this is human too now

human, the concern for
profit margins, efficacy,
emotional punch, whatever
is dredged with this
method. Take the slime-
vocabulary of observation

in its own cold equality
from which the bones
can be pasted into what

wherein the hypothesis
intent disappearing is
the intent to abrade
the superfluous, which is to
the synaptic, the choice,
a leap from body

which is pregnant with
complete calm of mind:
call it science;
the periosteum evening to
bare air-weight bone,
in principle abraded

so what is left is lewd:
voluptuously willing to
correlate, unveiling every
simplicity of this cheap
purse in which you put this
new version of being

sheerly effective
with strictest liberty,
whose aim is unrestricted
intelligence. We will use this
the black slum of data
whose final aim is capital

and freedom, the avenue
without feeling or concern,
happenstance or intention,

feints at humanity, but
grips like a lover, clothed in
familiarity, to whom one is
completely incidental

a city of cause and effect,
traffic that flows through
a possible street
like water, like open flesh.

MARSYAS

They are done with him. Leave
half eaten grapes on the floor
in the dark. The floor is cold.
I stand there remembering

half eaten grapes on the floor.
I was drunk on their closeness.
I stand there remembering
under the fluorescent lights.

I was drunk on their closeness.
It was as though I and not they
under the fluorescent lights
peeled off that skin.

It was as though I and not they
stepped forward and whispered to
that peeled off skin,
I did this I did this I

step forward and whisper to that
thing swaying from a hook
I did this I did this I
step back in silence.

Thing swaying from a hook.
We are done with him. Leave,
step back in silence
in the dark. The floor is cold.

"Electron Microscopy of a Blood Smear": Samples for electron microscopy require complete dehydration. This is usually accomplished by exposing samples to increasing concentrations of alcohol.

"Perfusion and Fixation of the Lungs": In this procedure, a 25-gauge needle is inserted into a slit that is made in the trachea, allowing a fixative to be injected directly into the lungs. This exposes tissue more thoroughly to the preservative, reducing degradation of the specimen.

"Dead Thing": Specimen carcasses are typically placed in a communal freezer before they are removed from the animal research facility and incinerated.

"Shut": Modifying metallic implants to release growth factors (e.g., bone morphogenetic protein, platelet-derived growth factor) can improve integration with the body. Growth of new bone can be assessed with histological stains such as Coomassie's blue.

"10. [In the end, the body could believe in little.]": Cells can be cryopreserved by freezing in a solution containing dimethyl sulfoxide (DMSO) and storing in liquid nitrogen. In the presence of DMSO, water at low temperatures adopts a glassy state and does not form ice crystals, which would otherwise puncture cell membranes and lead to necrosis.

"Semele and Dionysus, as Induced Pluripotent Stem Cell": Induced pluripotent stem cells (iPSC) have the capacity to develop into any and all types of tissue. One common method of assessing this ability is implanting iPSC into a living host, which leads to the formation of a disorganized mass of multiple tissue types, known as a teratoma.

"Abattoir": A common treatment for blood cancers such as leukemia is ablation of the patient's own bone marrow, followed by transplantation of donor bone marrow. Donor bone marrow can be derived from the patients themselves, usually with attendant procedures to remove cancerous cells, or from other individuals. Morbidity frequently accompanies transplants, due to low engraftment of donor cells. Leukemia patients often have pitted and brittle bones, due to cancerous marrow replacing strength-bearing osteocytes.

"The Spear of Achilles, as Gene Editing": Cas proteins are a bacterial defense mechanism that have been adapted for gene editing applications in mammalian cells, including humans. Experiments have recently been published describing gene editing of a human baby using Cas protein-based CRISPR.

"Sonnets": The first line is from Shakespeare's Sonnet 146.

"Blast": A -blast cell is a progenitor cell capable of developing into multiple cell types. Cells that form strong attachments to a substrate may grow on tissue culture-treated plastic plates, in which they form connections with the plastic via integrin cell membrane proteins, as well as cytoskeletal elements such as actin. Cells kept for too long in culture may overgrow and die.

ACKNOWLEDGMENTS

Grateful acknowledgment is made to the editors of the following
journals in which versions of these poems first appeared:

Colorado Review: "After Francis Bacon"

Conjunctions: "1. [The knowledge we gathered is no longer useful.],"
"2. [They have invented poems with algorithms.]," "8. [That which
is given but cannot be owned:]," "10. [In the end, the body could
believe in little.]," and "11. [Matter is ongoing   in widening
distances.]"

Denver Quarterly: "3. [Before I get to the two trees.]"

Ecdysis: "Sonnets"

Lana Turner: "Mouse," "Track," "Euthanasia," and "Semele and
Dionysus, as Induced Pluripotent Stem Cell"

Nat. Brut: "Bird" and "Jiangning"

New American Writing: "On the Mechanical Properties of Frozen Flesh"

Omniverse: "Job"

Pangyrus: "Lab Mouse Litany"

Peripheries Journal: "Subject"

The Road Not Taken: "(I left the lab) (I walked across the" [from "Sonnets"]

My thanks to Dan Kaplan and Sid Miller at Burnside Review Press, as well as Darcie Dennigan for selecting my work. My heartfelt gratitude to my teachers and mentors Peter Richards, Jorie Graham, and David Mooney, as well as family, colleagues, and friends who were generous with their time and spirit. I would furthermore like to acknowledge the National Institutes of Health and National Science Foundation for their support of the scientific research activities mentioned in this book.

Angelo Mao is a research scientist. He earned his Ph.D. in bioengineering from Harvard University. His first book, *Abattoir*, was selected by Darcie Dennigan as the winner of the 2019 Burnside Review Press Book Award. He was born in California and lives in Massachusetts.